*FIND IT FAST **FIND IT FAST** FIND IT FAST*

BIBLE
PROMISES

Instant Help in Times of Need

THOMAS NELSON PUBLISHERS
© Copyright 2001. Thomas Nelson, Inc.
ISBN: 0-7852-4755-6

Find it Fast

What to remember when you feel...

Abandoned
God is always with you. —Isaiah 41:10
You are sheltered in God's arms. —Deuteronomy 33:27
Nothing can separate you from God's love. —Romans 8:35-39
God will take care of you. —Psalm 27:10
God cares for you. —1 Peter 5:6-7

Afraid
God hasn't given you a spirit of fear. —2 Timothy 1:7
You will not be in bondage to fear. —Romans 8:15-16
You will not be afraid of terror in the night. —Psalm 91:5-11
God is by your side. —Hebrews 13:5-6
God will give you His peace. —John 14:27

Angry
Slow-tempered people have great understanding. —Proverbs 14:17, 29
Those who are slow to anger are better than the mighty. —Proverbs 16:32
Anger leads to foolishness. —Ecclesiastes 7:9
Don't let the sun go down on your anger. —Ephesians 4:26
Be slow to wrath. —James 1:19-20

Anxious
Your nights won't be filled with worries, but with pleasant dreams.
—Proverbs 3:24
God cares for your needs because you are precious to him.
—Matthew 6:25-34
Jesus promised you peace of mind and of heart. —John 14:27
You will lie down in peace, able to sleep. —Psalm 4:8

Ashamed
The shadow of shame will be changed to joy when you look to God.
—Psalm 34:5
When you obey God's Word, your life will not become a disgrace.
—Psalm 119:6
Your salvation by Jesus Christ is nothing to be ashamed of.
—Romans 1:16
Do not be ashamed when you are persecuted for your faith.
—Ezekiel 36:23
Your upright conduct will put your accusers to shame. —I Peter 3:14-16

BIBLE PROMISES

CONDEMNED

When you belong to Jesus, there is no longer any condemnation.
—Romans 8:1

God blots out your sins and never thinks about them again.
—Isaiah 43:25

You will never be condemned for your sins once you are forgiven.
—John 5:24

You are a whole new person, and the old life is gone.
—2 Corinthians 5:17

There is no judgment awaiting those who trust in Jesus. —John 3:16-18

Jesus will forgive your sins and will not condemn you for them.
—John 8:10,11

CONFUSED

Though you may become perplexed, don't give up.
—2 Corinthians 4:8-10

God will direct you on the paths you should follow. —Proverbs 3:5-6

No matter what you may be facing, God is right there with you.
—Isaiah 43:2

Don't worry, but pray about everything. —Philippians 4:6,7

Ask God what He wants you to do, and He will gladly tell you.
—James 1:5

DEJECTED

Jesus understands all your weaknesses and temptations.
—Hebrews 4:15-16

Call to God, and He will answer you. —Jeremiah 33:3

God is merciful when we cry for help, even if we don't deserve it.
—Daniel 9:18

God will make you His own. —Jeremiah 24:7

Draw close to God, and He will draw close to you.
—James 4:8

If you look for God, you will find Him. —Jeremiah 29:13

DEPRESSED

When you are drowning in your troubles, God is with you.
—Isaiah 43:2

Though your night is filled with tears, joy will come in the morning.
—Psalm 30:5

God can change your times of depression into joy. —Isaiah 61:3

God is the source of your comfort. —2 Corinthians 1:3, 4

Find it Fast

Don't be sad, for the joy of the Lord is your strength.
—Nehemiah 8:10

Despair

God can change your despair into songs of praise. —Isaiah 61:3

God's love for you is unfailing. —Psalm 100:5

Nothing is too hard for God. —Jeremiah 32:17

God gives power to you when you are tired and worn out.
—Isaiah 40:29

God will not allow your hope to be crushed. —Psalm 119:116

Despondent

Don't become troubled, but trust God. —John 14:1

Though you are pressed by your troubles, don't give up.
—2 Corinthians 4:8-9

Though you face difficulties, there is a wonderful joy ahead.
—I Peter 1:6-9

God has begun a good work in your life, and He will finish it.
—Philippians 1:6

Trust in God, be strong and take courage. —Psalm 31:24

Disappointed

Jesus will grant your requests. —John 15:7

God knows your hopes. —Psalm 10:17

God will answer your prayers. —Mark 11:24

God can accomplish more than we would even think to hope.
—Ephesians 3:20

Discouraged

Your discouragement will be replaced by joy and gladness.
—Isaiah 51:11

Your trust in God will bring you great reward. —Hebrews 10:35,36

God will be your helper in the midst of your troubles. —Psalm 27:9

Put your hope in God, leaving discouragement behind.
—Psalm 42:11

When you wait upon the Lord, you will find new strength.
—Isaiah 40:30-31

Disheartened

God is with you through all your troubles. —Isaiah 43:2

Though you cry all night long, joy will come in the morning.
—Psalm 30:5

BIBLE PROMISES

God will give you new strength. —Isaiah 40:31

Our fears about today cannot separate us from God's love.
—Romans 8:38-39

God heals the brokenhearted. —Psalm 147:3

God cares about what happens to you. —I Peter 5:6-7

DISOBEDIENT

Those who obey Christ remain in His love. —John 15:10

If you really love God, you will obey His commandments. —1 John 2:5

Happiness is found on the path of obedience. —Psalm 119:35

True disciples of Jesus will obey His teachings. —John 8:31-32

God will make His home with those who obey His Word. —John 14:23

DISSATISFIED

God will give you the desires of your heart. —Psalm 37:4

God can satisfy more than the richest of foods. —Psalm 63:1-5

God will fill your life with good things. —Psalm 103:1-5

God will satisfy you with His love. —Psalm 90:14

We will be fully satisfied when we see God face to face. —Psalm 17:15

DOUBTFUL

If you have no doubt in your heart, God will answer your prayers.
—Mark 11:22-24

All of God's promises will prove true. —Psalm 18:30

FAILURE

God will hold you in His victorious hand. —Isaiah 41:10

Nothing you do for the Lord is ever useless —1 Corinthians 15:58

God will provide you with a rich treasure when He returns.
—Isaiah 33:6

You are strong because God is with you wherever you go. —Joshua 1:9

God knows your motives and will give you due praise.
—1 Corinthians 4:3-5

FINANCIALLY STRAPPED

God will care for your needs. —Psalm 23:1

God will bless you with all you need if you obey Him.
—Deuteronomy 28:2-13

God knows your needs and will provide for you day to day.
—Matthew 6:31-33

God will supply all of your needs. —Philippians 4:19

God will provide for all that you need and more. —2 Corinthians 9:6-8

Find it Fast

Forsaken
God sees your heart. —1 Samuel 16:7
If you seek God, you will find Him. —1 Chronicles 28:9
You who delight in the Lord will be made to prosper. —Psalm 1:1-3
Overwhelming victory is ours through Jesus Christ. —Romans 8:37
God will help you when everything is going against you.
—Psalm 37:5-7
God has chosen you for His own and forgiven you. —Colossians 3:12-14

Frantic and Stressed
God is wonderfully good to those who wait for Him.
—Lamentations 3:25-26
Wait patiently for the Lord. —Psalm 27:14
When you wait patiently for God, He hears your prayers. —Psalm 40:1
These tests that come your way will strengthen your character.
—James 1:2-4
These trials will show that your faith is strong and pure. —1 Peter 1:7

Frustrated
Show love for one another, for love covers a multitude of sins.
—1 Peter 4:8
Don't react with anger and harsh words, but forgive.
—Ephesians 4:31-32
Stop your anger, turn from your rage, and God will help you.
—Psalm 37:8-9
God can help you control your words or keep your mouth shut.
—Psalm 141:3

Grieving
God blesses the mourner, and He will comfort them. —Matthew 5:4
God has everlasting comfort for your heart. —2 Thessalonians 2:16-17
God has given you victory over sin and death.
—1 Corinthians 15:55-57
There will be no more death or sorrow or crying or pain.
—Revelation 21:4
Cling to Jesus because He understands all your weakness.
—Hebrews 4:14-15
God is close by your side, protecting and comforting you. —Psalm 23:4
Jesus is preparing a place for you and will return for you.
—John 14:1-3

Bible Promises

Guilty
You have been made right with God because of Jesus.
—1 Corinthians 6:11

God is a God of forgiveness; slow to anger and full of mercy.
—Nehemiah 9:17

God keeps no record of our sins. —Psalm 130:3-4

God will cleanse away all of your sins and rebellion. —Jeremiah 33:8

There is no judgment awaiting you because you trust in God.
—John 3:18

God blots out our sins and never gives them another thought.
—Isaiah 43:25

Impatient
Wait on the Lord and you will find new strength. —Isaiah 40:31

It is good to wait quietly. —Lamentations 3:26

God will fulfill all of His promises to those who wait patiently.
—Hebrews 10:35-37

God gives us patience and encouragement. —Romans 15:4-5

Wait patiently for the Lord and He will turn towards you. —Psalm 40:1

Inferior
The Holy Spirit will help you in your distress. —Romans 8:26-27

God's love for you is so great. —Ephesians 3:17-19

Trust God with confidence, no matter what happens. —Hebrews 10:35-36

God has begun a good work in you, and He will complete it.
—Philippians 1:6

God listens to you whenever you talk to him. —1 John 5:14-15

Insecure
Jesus will never change. —Hebrews 13:18

God has promised you a wonderful future. —Ephesians 1:18-19

The fruit of your life will bring much glory and praise to God.
—Philippians 1:9-11

The words of Christ living in your hearts will make you wise.
—Colossians 3:16

God will keep you and care for you until Jesus returns. —John 17:11

God will fill you with power and help you to understand.
—Ephesians 3:18-19

Find it Fast

Lonely
Jesus is always with you. —Matthew 28:20
God is with you, and He will help and strengthen you. —Isaiah 41:10
God goes in front of you, and He will never fail you.
　—Deuteronomy 31:6
God is your refuge, and He holds you in His arms.—Deuteronomy 33:27

Longing
God will fill your desires. —Psalm 145:19
God can turn your eyes from worthless things. —Psalm 119:37
Crave spiritual things so that you grow in your salvation.
　—1 Peter 2:2
Desire the spiritual gifts. —I Corinthians 14:1

Perplexed
Ask God what He wants you to do, and He will gladly tell you.
　—James 1:5
God is not a God of disorder but of peace. —1 Corinthians 14:33
God will tell you when to turn and where to walk. —Isaiah 30:21
Don't worry over things, but pray and He will give you peace.
　—Philippians 4:6-7
God will guide you along the best pathway for your life. —Psalm 32:8

Persecuted
The kingdom of heaven belongs to those who are persecuted.
　—Matthew 5:10
The trials you find yourself in will bring you a share of glory.
　—1 Peter 4:12-13
God will give justice when you are treated unfairly. —Psalm 103:6
God will deliver you from your oppressors. —Jeremiah 20:13
God hears the prayers of the righteous. —1 Peter 3:11-12
God's unfailing love will surround you when you trust Him.
　—Psalm 32:10

Rebellious
Rebellion is sin, and stubbornness is like idol worship.
　—1 Samuel 15:22-23
Let your attitude be the same as Christ Jesus. —Philippians 2:5-8
God shows favor to those who submit to their elder's authority.
　—1 Peter 5:5-6
Use your whole body as a tool to do what is right. —Romans 6:12-13

BIBLE PROMISES

Your behavior should match your position as a child of light.
—Ephesians 5:8

Remorseful

If you confess your sins to God, He is faithful to forgive you.
—1 John 1:9

Those who believe will never be condemned for their sins. —John 5:24

God will blot out your sins and never give them another thought.
—Isaiah 43:25

Your evil conscience has been made clean by Christ's blood.
—Hebrews 10:22

If you return to God, He will welcome you and have mercy.
—2 Chronicles 30:9

Sick

A prayer offered in faith will heal the sick. —James 5:14-15

God in His mercy can heal your illnesses. —Philippians 2:25-30

God can heal you, snatching you from death's door.
—Psalm 107:20

We have been healed by Jesus' wounds. —1 Peter 2:24

God is able to forgive sins and heal diseases. —Psalm 103:3

Suffering

The trials we face bring us joy, for they strengthen our character.
—Romans 5:3-4

If you suffer for doing right, God will reward you for it. —1 Peter 3:14

Though you face many troubles, God will rescue you. —Psalm 34:19

If you suffer patiently for doing right, God is pleased with you.
—1 Peter 2:20-21

Shall we accept the good things and never anything bad? —Job 2:10

Christians all over the world are suffering just like you. —1 Peter 5:8-9

Tempted

Hide God's Word in your heart so that you won't sin against Him.
—Psalm 119:11

Jesus faced all the same temptations that we do. —Hebrews 4:14-16

God will keep temptations from being stronger than you.
—1 Corinthians 10:12-13

Vengeful

God will carry out His furious vengeance. —Ezekiel 25:12-17

God will take vengeance. He will repay. —Hebrews 10:30

Find it Fast

God will take vengeance upon His enemies. —Jeremiah 46:9-10

God will bring judgment. —2 Thessalonians 1:8

Weak

When you are overwhelmed, God knows where you should turn. —Psalm 142:3

God is your strength. —Habakkuk 3:19

Search for the Lord and for His strength. —1 Chronicles 16:11

God's strength is made perfect in your weakness. —2 Corinthians 12:9

What the Bible has to say about...

Blessings

God will send out showers of blessings. —Ezekiel 34:26

God has blessed you with every spiritual blessing. —Ephesians 1:3

God has stored up great blessings for those who honor Him. —Psalm 31:19

God blesses those who trust Him and put their hope in Him. —Jeremiah 17:7

Care

God will water your life like a garden when you are dry. —Isaiah 58:11

God cares for all of your needs. —Psalm 23:1

God is the one who keeps you alive. —Psalm 54:4

Don't worry about everyday life; God will care for your needs. —Matthew 6:25-27

God will provide generously for your every need. —2 Corinthians 9:8

Comfort

You belong to God and He holds your hand. —Psalm 73:23-24

Jesus is with you always. —Matthew 28:20

Jesus will never reject you when you come to Him. —John 6:37

God will hold you close, no matter who else abandons you. —Psalm 27:10

Death

You were once doomed because of your sins. —Ephesians 2:1

You have been raised up to a new life. —Colossians 2:12-13

Anyone who obeys Jesus' teachings will never die. —John 8:51

The godly have a refuge when they die. —Proverbs 14:27, 32

You already have been given eternal life. —John 5:21-24

Bible Promises

Discipleship
A student isn't greater than his teacher, but can be like the teacher. —Luke 6:40

If you give your life for Jesus, you will find true life. —Luke 9:23-26

If you follow after Jesus, God will honor you. —John 12:26

Knowing Jesus is a priceless gain. —Philippians 3:8-9

Discipline
God disciplines those that He loves. —Proverbs 3:11-12

God will not allow those who need discipline to go unpunished. —Jeremiah 30:11

Just like a parent, God disciplines you to help you. —Deuteronomy 8:5

Discipline yields a quiet harvest of right living. —Hebrews 12:11

God corrects and disciplines everyone that He loves. —Revelation 3:19

The correction of discipline is the way to life. —Proverbs 6:23

Encouragement
God knows His plans for your life: for hope and a future. —Jeremiah 29:11

God has given you everlasting comfort and hope. —2 Thessalonians 2:16-17

The Lord knows how to rescue you from your trials. —2 Peter 2:9

God will work out His plans for your life. —Psalm 138:8

God is not unfair. He will not forget the good you have done. —Hebrews 6:10

Eternal Life
God has given you eternal life in His Son. —1 John 5:11-12

Your heart will rejoice with an everlasting joy. —Psalm 22:26

You will live in the house of the Lord forever. —Psalm 23:6

Jesus brought the gift of eternal life. —John 4:13-14

Everyone who believes in Jesus already has eternal life. —John 6:47

Jesus is the resurrection and the life. —John 11:25-26

Faith
You can be confident that what you hope for is going to happen. —Hebrews 11:1

Faith comes by listening to the gospel. —Romans 10:17

God rewards those who seek Him in faith. —Hebrews 11:6

Your faith is precious to God. —1 Peter 1:7

Anything is possible if a person believes. —Mark 9:23

Find it Fast

Faithfulness of God
God's faithfulness is as enduring as the heavens. —Psalm 89:1-2, 33-34
Of all His wonderful promises, not one word has failed. —1 Kings 8:56
Even if you are unfaithful, God remains faithful. —2 Timothy 2:13, 19
God is faithful. —1 Corinthians 10:13

Fellowship
Your love for other Christians will show you are a Christian.
—John 13:34-35
Love your neighbor. —Romans 13:8
Where two or three are gathered, God is among them. —Matthew 18:20
All Christians are one in Jesus. —Galatians 3:28
Love one another sincerely, with all your hearts. —1 Peter 1:22

Forgiveness
God is ready to forgive you. —Psalm 86:5
Your sins have been removed as far as the east is from the west.
—Psalm 103:12
When you stop trying to hide your sin and confess, God forgives.
—Psalm 32:5-6
If you confess your sin, God will forgive you. —1 John 1:9
God pardons your sins because He delights in showing mercy.
—Micah 7:18-19
Your sins will be forgiven through Jesus' name. —Acts 10:43

Freedom
If Jesus sets you free, you will indeed be free. —John 8:34-36
By God's grace you are free from the power of sin. —Romans 6:14
You are no longer a slave to sin. —Romans 6:6

Grace of God
God gives you grace. —Psalm 84:11
God gives you the grace you need when you most need it.
—Hebrews 4:16
God's grace will continue to bring people to Christ. —2 Corinthians 4:15

Guidance
God will lead you with unfailing love into His holiness. —Exodus 15:13
God will direct your paths. —Proverbs 3:6
The Holy Spirit will teach you and will guide you. —John 14:26
God's Spirit within you is what makes you wise. —Job 32:8-9
God's Spirit will guide you forward on firm footing. —Psalm 143:10

BIBLE PROMISES

HOLINESS
When you stand before God, Jesus makes you holy.
—1 Thessalonians 3:13

You must be holy because God is holy. —Leviticus 20:7

You were chosen to be holy and blameless in His eyes. —Ephesians 1:4

Jesus' power gives us all we need for holy living. —2 Peter 1:3

We are made right with God through Jesus. —2 Corinthians 5:21

HOLY SPIRIT
Your body is the temple of the Holy Spirit. —1 Corinthians 6:19

God shows His love for you by giving you His Holy Spirit.
—Romans 5:5

The Spirit is your Counselor, who will never leave you. —John 14:16-17

Jesus came baptizing with the Holy Spirit. —Matthew 3:11

The Holy Spirit comes upon those who believe in Jesus. —Acts 19:2-6

HOPE
We have a living hope because Jesus is risen. —1 Peter 1:3

Look forward with hope to the day when Jesus will return. —Titus 2:13

Your hope in God is like a strong anchor for your soul. —Hebrews 6:19

Your only hope is in God. —Psalm 39:7

JOY
The joy of the Lord is your strength. —Nehemiah 8:10

Your joy will overflow because you remain in God's love.
—John 15:10-11

God fills you with joy and peace. —Romans 15:13

Joy will be yours when you do what is right. —Psalm 97:11

LOVE
Your love for your fellow Christians will prove your discipleship.
—John 13:34-35

God's love for you is everlasting and unfailing. —Jeremiah 31:3

God has showed you great love. —Romans 5:8

God loves you so much that He gave up His only son for you.
—John 3:16

Nothing can separate you from God's love for you. —Romans 8:37-39

OBEDIENCE
Your obedience is more pleasing to God than any sacrifice.
—1 Samuel 15:22

Obedience to God leads to peace and righteousness. —Isaiah 48:17-18

Find it Fast

Obedience to your leaders will be rewarded by God later.
—Colossians 3:20-25

Peace

We have peace with God because of Jesus. —Romans 5:1-2

God will keep you in perfect peace. —Isaiah 26:3-4

Righteousness will bring peace and quietness and confidence.
—Isaiah 32:17

In serving Jesus, you will find rest for your soul. —Matthew 11:29

Peace of mind and peace of heart are a gift from Jesus. —John 14:27

Praise

Singing praises to God is delightful and right. —Psalm 147:1

You will praise the Lord all the time. —Psalm 34:1-3

Praise the Lord with psalms and hymns and spiritual songs.
—Ephesians 5:18-20

You will always find yourself praising the Lord. —Psalm 71:5-8

Prayer

Keep asking and you will be given what you ask for. —Matthew 7:7

The ears of the Lord are always open to your prayers. —1 Peter 3:12

God is listening to you whenever you ask Him for something.
—1 John 5:14-15

God answers your prayers. —Psalm 65:2-5

Return of Christ

Jesus will return. —1 Thessalonians 4:13-18

Jesus will return unexpectedly, like a thief in the night.
—2 Peter 3:3-4, 8-13

You are looking forward to that wonderful event: Jesus' return.
—Titus 2:11-13

Jesus will arrive in the clouds with great power and glory.
—Luke 21:25-28

Salvation

To all who believed, God gave salvation. —John 1:12

Jesus will give you eternal life, which no one can take away.
—John 10:28

God has given you eternal life in His Son. —1 John 5:11-12

Jesus was able to provide salvation once and for all. —Hebrews 7:25

Everyone who believes in Jesus already has eternal life. —John 6:47

Your salvation was purchased with the blood of Jesus. —Ephesians 1:7

BIBLE PROMISES

SATAN
Stand firm against the attacks of the devil. —1 Peter 5:8-9
Resist the devil and he will flee from you. —James 4:7-8
God will help you stand firm against the tricks of the devil.
—Ephesians 6:10-18
God will help you to win your battle with Satan. —1 John 2:12-14

SERVING GOD
Serve God by finding ways to serve one another. —Romans 12:10-13
Whoever wants to lead will become the servant of all.
—Matthew 20:26-28
Serve God with all your heart and all your soul. —Joshua 22:5
Serve only God. Listen to His voice and cling to Him.
—Deuteronomy 13:4

STEWARDSHIP
If you are put in charge of something, you must be faithful.
—1 Corinthians 4:1-2
Manage the gifts you have been given well. —1 Peter 4:10-11
We must explain to God all that we have done. —Hebrews 4:13
Don't store up treasures here on earth; they will only get rusty.
—Matthew 6:19
If you give, you will receive in full measure. —Luke 6:38

STRENGTH
God is your strength and your song. —Isaiah 12:2
God gives His people strength. —Psalm 29:11
God will steady you and make you strong. —Psalm 89:21
Jesus will give you the strength you need. —Philippians 4:13

THOUGHTS
God knows your every thought. —Psalm 139:2
God knows your innermost thoughts and desires. —Hebrews 4:12
God searches out your heart and knows your very thoughts.
—Psalm 139:23
God will forgive your evil thoughts when you ask Him to. —Acts 8:22

TRUST
You can trust in God's holy name. —Psalm 33:21
When you trust God, you will never be disappointed. —Psalm 22:4-5
Trust God and He will help you. —Psalm 37:3, 5
Trust in the Lord with all your heart. —Proverbs 3:5-6

Find it Fast   7-12-03

TRUTH
You will know the truth and the truth will set you free. —John 8:31-32
The truth will make you pure and holy. —John 17:17-19
Hold to the truth in love, and you will become more like Christ.
   —Ephesians 4:15
Stand firm in the truth. —2 Peter 1:12

VICTORY
You can do everything with the help of Christ. —Philippians 4:13
You can trust Christ to give the victory. —1 John 5:4
Jesus will be victorious. —Psalm 110:7
Jesus will return and have the final victory. —Revelation 19:11-21

WAITING
Wait quietly for the Lord. —Psalm 62:1, 5
God is good to those who wait for Him. —Lamentations 3:25-26
Wait for the Lord and He will hear your cry. —Psalm 40:1
Be courageous while you wait patiently for the Lord. —Psalm 27:14

WILL OF GOD
If you do the will of God, Jesus is your brother. —Matthew 12:50
It is the will of God that Jesus not lose anyone who is His.
   —John 6:39-40
God's will is good and pleasing and perfect. —Romans 12:2
May God's will be done on earth. —Matthew 6:10

WISDOM
The Spirit of God gives great wisdom. —Exodus 31:3
The fear of the Lord is the beginning of wisdom. —Proverbs 9:10
When you are obedient, others will say you are wise.
   —Deuteronomy 4:6
God will give you wisdom and the right words to say. —Luke 21:15
The Spirit gives some the ability to give wise advice. —1 Corinthians 12:8
God will give you spiritual wisdom and understanding.
   —Ephesians 1:17
If you need wisdom, ask God to give it to you. —James 1:5

ZEAL
You should have a zeal to see others saved. —Romans 10:1
You will have the zeal to do what is right. —2 Corinthians 7:11
You should be zealous to have spiritual gifts. —1 Corinthians 14:12
You shall have a zeal to do the right thing. —Titus 2:14